GMW
Architects

Creativity and Urban Development

Preface by
Terry Brown
Introduction by
Maurizio Vogliazzo

l'ARCAEDIZIONI

Acknowledgement
*In a partnership such as GMW Architects, projects
become very much a matter of shared authorship and
responsibility, with the expertise of many personalities
being brought to bear in different ways through
the equally important stages of design, critique, design
development and construction. To credit all those who
played a part in the work of the practice during these
years would cover many densely printed pages.
The current partners acknowledge the input of their
retired colleagues and of the many talented
collaborators who worked on the projects included
here, thank them, and express the hope that, though
not individually credited, they will feel able to take
pride in the projects to which their
contribution was often crucial.*

*On two projects GMW Architects collaborated with
other designers. The St Enoch Centre team included
Reiach and Hall in Edinburgh and retail design from
HOK of St Louis, while at Milton Keynes Greg and
Stephenson worked on the shopping mall interiors.
On both these projects the conceptual design and
design team leadership was GMW's responsibility.*

Chief Editor of Collection
Maurizio Vitta

Publishing Coordinator
Franca Rottola

Editorial Staff
Cristina Rota

Graphic Design
Paola Polastri

Editing and Translation
Martyn J. Anderson

Colour-separation
LitofilmsItalia, Bergamo

Printing
Bolis Poligrafiche Spa, Azzano San Paolo (BG)

First published October 2003

ISBN 88-7838-123-3

Contents

Preface

by Terry Brown

The projects included here have been selected from the work of GMW Architects completed over a period of almost three decades, between 1975 and 2002. It was a time of considerable change, both in architecture and in the building industry.

We experienced the building boom of the eighties and suffered from the recession of the nineties. We saw the waxing and waning of Postmodernism and in the UK the devastating effects of terrorist activity in the City of London and elsewhere. Energy shortages at the beginning of the seventies and the threat of resource depletion preceded the discovery of global warming and the emergence of the environmental movement. At the end of this period, with the dawning of the twenty first century, the way we build, the state of the environment and the direction of architecture still, as ever, pose interesting questions. For GMW, this has been a period of intense creativity, building on an approach to design forged during the era of Gollins, Melvin and Ward, adapting it to changing circumstances, but importantly, also often challenging it.

With hindsight it is interesting to note that certain themes reoccur in these projects. A preoccupation with the technology of the metal and glass curtain wall and its potential to create a sense of lightness and an uninterrupted connection between inside and outside has influenced even the stone clad buildings featured here. The development of the atrium or the sheltered urban space, public or apparently public, can also be traced through these projects, each of which in its own way makes an important contribution to the public realm.

We have a strong tradition of using technology in an understated way. Repetition of details allows refinement and we have disciplined ourselves to exploit the true advantages of machine production rather than exaggerate it unnecessarily, or symbolise it with what are, in reality, highly crafted components. Our buildings have all been achieved within the constraints of tight commercial budgets. We have aimed for a robust kind of simplicity that can stand the test of time. We advocate a universality of forms and an adaptable arrangement of space that allows changing patterns of use during the life of our buildings.

It is interesting to compare buildings such as Equitable Life, Aylesbury and Zurich Insurance, Portsmouth, designed in the mid seventies and early eighties, with what others and we are doing currently. Today clearer high performance glasses are favoured, achieving more transparency than their tinted or mirror coated predecessors and out-rigged or other forms of solar control reflect an increasing concern for energy conservation; fashions in colour and finish change, but the underlying technology and overarching aesthetic has remained mostly the same.

Within our genre, though, we have not been fearful of experiment. Most notably, during the eighties, when we became concerned that our earlier buildings started to seem, in some ways, bland or over rationalised and maybe even inhuman.

Also, like others we began to regret the erosion of our historic cities. This set us on a course to try to emulate the complexity of the historic city in individual new buildings, which at the time seemed to be growing ever larger in scale.

Our experiments with highly articulated, but still modular building forms and historical references in the details were intended to avoid pastiche, but rather to give new buildings humanity and character, setting them more effectively into the existing fabric of the city.

54 Lombard Street and Minster Court both tackle these design ambitions. Supposedly because it is demanding of the collective resource, there has always been a concern for seriousness in architecture and, after the initial euphoria, there was a fairly deep reaction against Postmodernism, with its apparent lack of integrity. This has sometimes clouded the fact that these buildings never really tried to be other than honestly of their time. A closer look at their detailing makes this clear.

The search for a humane architecture continued in later projects, but with a renewed concern for constructional integrity and perhaps even just a little forelock tugging toward our critics! Two important factors entered in and changed our attitude towards history and our approach to design within the urban context. These were the terrorist attacks in the City of London and the groundswell of conservation, with the increasingly likely requirement that historic building fabric be incorporated within new developments. Now, sites would often not be entirely cleared, but only partially, with new fabric integrated carefully with existing elements, sometimes for practical and economic reasons but often to conserve historical or architectural interest.

Seen in combination with historic fabric, new work has to follow one of two opposite courses: either legitimate restoration, or complementary intervention, honestly and explicitly of its time.

Our work on Tower 42 saw a complete refurbishment of an iconic building only completed some twenty years earlier, reinstating the original appearance, save for a completely redesigned three storey entrance hall of stainless steel and glass. At 16 Old Bailey an incomplete Edwardian pavilion has been adapted and completed with new hand carved natural stone but combined with new office space clad in clear and opaque glass and aluminium. This was a way back to our modernist roots, but with lessons learnt, that emerged with a renewed confidence in Atatürk Air Terminal. Here we have restated our commitment to continuity and simplicity of space, calmness of detail, quality of finishes and above all the celebration of daylight.

The value of a retrospective is partly to take stock of past achievements, but also partly to gauge what pointers may be found to the future. There are surely some within these projects!

At the dawn of the twenty first century we must anticipate further huge changes in our lives. On the one hand science and technology deliver new possibilities that challenge our most fundamental beliefs about life and lifestyle, while on the other we are becoming acutely aware of the interacting but ultimately closed systems of our planet and the devastating effects twentieth century technology has had on climate, natural resources, biodiversity and the global balance of human wealth and poverty.

With each new project, these issues are reconsidered, though we will inevitably build on our own direct experience. St Enoch Centre pioneered a passively tempered day-lit enclosure. 16 Old Bailey integrates historic and modern fabric in a way that creates a continuity with the past but without compromising current tenant expectations. Atatürk airport eases the stress of travelling with easily navigated, airy, light-filled public concourses. Midsummer Place shopping centre incorporates a strong day-lit public focus. And all the projects featured here employ materials in a refined and minimalist way that eschews waste. But most importantly, each of these projects demonstrates a design approach that seeks to breath new life into cities, either upfront with its visual quality or in the background, by providing the necessary facilities and a stimulating setting for urban life to flourish. These are mostly simple things, but rarely easy to achieve.

It is of course a fine balance between simplicity and complexity that makes the things we use in our daily lives more attractive and satisfying. In architecture and urban design, it is also the balance between conservation and renewal. Achieving these balances, combined with serving purpose effectively, efficiently and in a sustainable way, will continue to be GMW Architects' aspiration.

Creativity and Urban Development

by Maurizio Vogliazzo

Julius Posener (who studied architecture under Hans Poelzig and also worked in Berlin with Erich Mendelsohn, eventually devoting himself to a form of experimentation which it would be wrong to describe as strictly historical, since it was actually full of subtle observations, authentic illuminations in the Benjaminian sense of the word, and intriguingly precise thoughts and lines of reasoning on architectural design, later rendered not just in the form of essays but also conferences and even long letters in line with the best of high European tradition, now lost for ever) has always maintained (even before his Anfaenge des Funktionalismus) that the roots of functionalism lie in England. At first sight this would seem to be nothing new: back in 1936 Nikolaus Pevsner had suggested something similar when trying to find some leit-motif running through the pioneers of the Modern Movement, laying the foundations for a historiographic tradition which, after all, is still very much in vogue. Nevertheless, Posener's claim does not work along exactly the same lines: based on a carefully compiled case history, it is actually the very definition of the term functionalism that changes and becomes more precise, taking on fresh connotations. As Posener says, "A proper definition of functional architecture is bound to be rather approximate: it is the programme that dictates what can be seen. The construction, implementing the programme, is still recognisable. The result is architecture. The shafts are placed in such and such a position, the dimensions specified in the programme are kept to, openings are made where they are needed in the most effective way possible; the building is constructed using the right means, viz., meeting safety, durability and budget requirements and drawing on the best technological means at the architect's disposal… We point out everything we think needs doing, and nothing else is required. Architecture is inevitably the result of this way of working."

Simple functionalism reduced to its bare bones: compatible, if you like, with certain ideas of Ruskin, Pugin and Morris, but, as you can see, bereft of all ideological implications. Pure functionalism but never really set down with due clarity: after all, tradition, certainly not lacking in its own solid foundations, which has always seen architecture as an art form, has never allowed it.

Yet only the English really realised all this, although perhaps in various different ways and adopting what were apparently quite different approaches; but certainly on a continuing basis: and this way of seeing and doing things is still as firmly entrenched as ever, despite all the major socio-economic, political or technological upheavals that have taken place. Over a hundred years ago, C.F.A. Voysey wrote that: "As regards design, I suggest the following method: take note of everything the construction calls for, in order of importance; hence all the conditions a building must satisfy. These two lists lead to a third about materials." What more could an architect say about his work, particularly one who is so English in terms of his background and training, and hence not so easily influenced by enticing international fashions and trends? GMW

for instance, who are an interesting case in this respect, provide a constantly fine example of this in designing and building their architecture: among all the instances deserving a mention, it is certainly worth pointing out Banque Belge from 1977 and the headquarters of Baring Brothers right in the heart of the City of London from 1981. Even the rest of what Voysey had to say, which might at first seem to play all this down and be a sort of change in direction, is not so at all if we think about it more carefully (and it is hard to agree with Posener here, who sees all this is a limit), indeed it actually fits like a glove: "At this point we are bound to ask that age-old question: why, in general, are we doing this? The reason, the key, must be the key to a melody of thoughts, the key and rhythm for a song." Voysey was a brilliant architect: on an absolute scale of values, assuming I might dare to propose one, one of the very best over the last one hundred and fifty years: what else could he have said in all honesty and without falling into some ideological trap or other?

And even William Richard Lethaby, a less gifted architect but a theorist, historian and teacher without equal and less inclined to make sweeping statements, basically says the same, not in his "Aphorisms" ("Beauty is a necessary function of what is appropriate"), nor, to quote another example, in Architecture and Modern Life: "I would like to suggest constructing buildings along the lines of validity and overall intelligibility, such as: compliance to purpose, fine execution, function, moderation and reason to make them intelligible; accuracy, knowledge, majesty, seriousness, pleasantness, urbanity, vitality, boldness and humanity to make them adequate; perfection, discipline, forthrightness, honesty, duration, order, clarity and unity. A couple of dozen words from those that architecture critics should always use; …but I must admit I find it amusing to try and imagine what architecture magazines will do with this list of mine… At times, I really am afraid that this famous sense of humour of ours will kill us some day." Self-irony aside, GMW's approach, consistent down the years, again comes to mind, as in the case of their long and carefully gauged work for Sheffield. Anyway, magazines and journals have certainly made a meal of all this over the last ninety years; not to mention the mountain of books published and those sitting quietly round the corner waiting to appear; and then of course there is the staggering excess of theories and endless imitations that have never been very healthy for architecture and never will be. And the architectural scene has never really stood out for its sense of humour, and less so than ever these days. So be it. Anyway, it is worth mentioning Lethaby's suggestion to use "…..the best forms of modern culture as examples of the kind of spirit in which we must set about the business of improving our cities. Each of us must feel involved, and it must be treated as something between duty and play.

I invite you all to play the best game of all: make the towns orderly." A quote from Make the Towns Orderly written in 1916.

Years on, the topical nature of these thoughts is quite surprising; and once again GMW's works in the City of London, in some sense, show how they can actually be applied. The "forms of modern culture" which, way back in his day, Lethaby was entitled to take into account, were altogether quite something else; and "bringing order" to that blanket of inextricable complexity, with all its different degrees of physicalness, that is gradually condensing almost seamlessly around our planet, might now mean piercing our big cities and exacerbated cityscapes with infrastructures, to quote Rem Koolhaas, or create as many touching surfaces as possible; who knows?

Going back for one moment to those aspects we might describe as more strictly related to architectural design, it can be seen that this very English meaning of functionalism and the various forms in which it is rendered are clearly set down and examined in Hermann Muthesius's magnificent analysis entitled Das Englische Haus. But the fact that from Robert Kerr's "The Gentleman's House" to Philip Webb's big country houses and, most notably amongst others, houses designed by Eden Nesfield, Norman Shaw and M.H. Baillie Scott, the dimensions and lifestyles in play are quite incompatible with the brutal changes and drastic, irreversible reductions in size following the first world war, should not lead us to conclude that, after all, despite how interesting this way of seeing and doing things was, it was also inextricably linked to a general state of affairs that will never arise again. It would be equally inadvisable to try and find any rather unlikely direct connections and links: to provide a really obvious example, the "new architecture" developed in Germany between 1920-30 and corresponding means of design, have very little if anything to do with what went on in England; on the contrary, Belgium offers a more comparable situation, only on a much smaller scale and hence more adaptable to a densely built urban environment, take for instance Pompe or Bodson; needless to say, this sort of "Architekturgeist" only underwent very gradual, inevitable changes in England, without causing any real commotion. It would also be right to claim that this notion of functionalism only played a minor part in the modern movement, like various other ideas that were discarded and cast aside by distinctly German-style continental European rational functionalism, well protected and backed-up by the fire power of a whole barrage of favourable critics. This is one of the reasons why it is so interesting, and there is still plenty of work to be done regarding these points. There is no point, and it would not even be possible, to even try and sum up the history of English architecture in the 20th century. In actual fact, there is probably no summary to be made, even if we wanted to: as is inevitably the case when faced with diversity, something that, as we all know, neither critics nor historians are very fond of. In this respect, only Reyner Banham has had anything interesting to say, on the right wave length, notably in relation to the 1950s-60s. Now, as we attempt to place GMW's architecture in its appropriate historical setting, it is at least worth mentioning the period between the wars, so vital for grasping the basic connotations of this very solid and carefully worked-out professionalism unlike anything found in any other country. In a setting that might be sweepingly classified as art déco (in this way even Le Corbusier would have to be described as the greatest and most extraordinary art déco architect; and, after all, that would be a fair description if it were formulated in slightly different terms: LC was also the greatest art déco architect), this original functional approach takes on various different guises and forms to cater for different input at different times, without ever (or hardly ever) betraying its basic tenets. Sometimes, cases which are not so clear-cut are actually easier to read, as in the case of Oliver Hill or plenty of designs by Sir Owen Williams that speak for themselves; other cases, like, for example, H.S. Goodhart-Rendel, call for more careful attention, like for instance Hay's Wharf, and the means of projecting light through the interiors certainly must not be overlooked.

Even those cases that seem to part company most drastically with Anglo-Saxon tradition actually confirm how deeply rooted this approach is and how it can never really be subdued, as epitomised by Giles Gilbert Scott. Of course, as usual, you need to open your eyes if you want to see all this. Combining this design expertise with those powerful works of architecture built around that time between Woburn Place and Tottenhan Court Road in Bloomsbury, just to quote one example in the heart of London, we get a general picture of a notable range of skills stretching right across the board, capable of handling even large-scale designs while holding onto its own clear identity. Nowadays, fine instances of this come once again from GMW in tricky contexts: take, for example, Tower 42, which amongst other things tackles issues of sustainable growth. Difficult issues which can only be faced with a full awareness of the matters at hand. This is no easy matter and can only be tackled with notable foresight. And this is just what can instantly be detected in the same area much later on after the second world war right down to the nineteen-seventies in the architectural designs of Hodkingson, Martin and Denys Lasdun, who came up with their own rendition of similar procedures.

It is now clear that James Melvin, Frank Gollins and Edmund Ward set up the GMW Partnership in the late 1940s working along quite clear lines. Despite the odd new partner and change in generation, their business has carried on uninterruptedly, tending if anything to expand. An architectural legacy passed on from father to son, it might be said. But that is not the case: the constant change in members of the workshop certainly has not taken place "within the family", so to speak, but in terms of a genuine identifying with the underlying philosophy of design that has never been betrayed but merely updated with careful circumspection. This aspect certainly should not be underrated, in a certain sense taking us back to the line of thinking we mentioned earlier. Being able to take note, as it actually happens we might say, how things work, how a way of designing architecture can last despite such far-reaching changes and transformations as those that have taken place over the last twenty years. Right from when the firm won an important competition for the master plan of Sheffield University and on a world scene which, at the time, saw, rather simplistically, F.Ll. Wright on one side (who could ever forget Bruno Zevi and his organic architecture, that he loved so much?), and on the other an American version of German-style rationalism, say Mies van der Rohe (a school of thought which, assuming it ever really existed and for some unknown reason, also included Le Corbusier, who really had nothing to do with it), GMW opted for a clear-cut stereometric and constructive approach.

This very carefully gauged design method was definitively enshrined in the explanatory charts that accompanied each of the firm's works. We now know that this was not Mies's way of working, although for a long time many people naturally assumed it was. In this respect, in its very English way and hidden away behind striking forms, GMW devote plenty of attention to users, to the pleasure of being and working in carefully designed spaces that certainly are not lacking in aesthetic touches; taking careful note of and never losing track of the basic data and moving through a carefully controlled world of materials, constantly working with and enhancing their characteristic features. Bricks, granite, just a bit of concrete, excepting an excursion into brutalism with the BOAC Terminal at Kennedy Airport, and above all glass, lots of glass, and iron. It is worth remembering that for Ruskin construction was the moral part of architecture (Fischer said that "what is moral is always moral in itself"); and it is almost an acknowledgement that metal is needed for the architecture of the future, but not without fear and apprehension. The reasons for these preferences are complicated, come from way back and have deep roots, and there is no need to be constantly aware of them; as time goes by they make it possible to reach unthinkable levels of elegance in the same old setting. And this applies to either materials or ideas, it makes no difference. But how come such breathtaking metal structures of such great poetic force have been built in England? Certainly not by following fashion trends, flailing around or copying. Or just by taking a gambol. Is high-tech the key?

You must be joking. Here expertise is deeply rooted. GMW have kept on working along these lines. There have been no doubts or about-turns: if anything, just ventures into sculptural designs like, for instance, in their interesting New Covent Garden Market. After working away patiently for years, GMW's mastery of their chosen materials lets them take experimentation to the very extremes, as in the Equitable Life Building, a notable exploration into the potential of curtain walls based on Euclidean expressionism, if we can use such an expression, carefully checked

and controlled to ensure it works properly. Or they play down prismatic rigidity even by creating something heavier, as in the case of Zurich Insurance.

The challenges are now getting even tougher; and in some respects even inevitable. It is hard, for instance, despite being free from the influence of contextualism and closely related continental historicism (who has ever heard of a British neo-liberty style?), to resist the pressure of history that has come so powerfully back into play, and in such an ambiguous manner, with the end of prohibition proposed by Paolo Portoghesi. We would rather refer to this and to the corresponding Venice Biennial of the 1980s, instead of lumping everything together under the heading of postmodernism (the "postmodern condition" comes from Lyotard and is not exactly the same thing). Pressure that is increased even more by a gradual spread in conservative prescriptions, which, when free from ideology, as is often the case, actually make some sense (although rather tardily).

It is also hard to safeguard against an irruption of urban issues related to unusual scales and settings, and complicated uses that are hard to decipher, extremely mixed uses and clients that overlap. This latter case was handled brilliantly: first the St Enoch Centre in Glasgow and then the Midsummer Place right in the middle of Milton Keynes, belonging to the latest generation of new towns, the former huge in size and the latter rather smaller but still a powerful presence, turn into well-tempered works of architecture, huge public spaces with their own easily recognisable form.

Gradually developing better control over micro-climatic conditions in search of that sustainability that is turning into the underlying premise for any further growth. In both cases, the procedure followed is perfectly in line with what English functionalist tradition requires; this ensures its success without having to resort, reluctantly, to alien methods with a logic of their own, such as plazas from overseas or urban furbishing from the continent. And the same old materials are hung onto and actually turn out to be particularly suited to problems of this scale.

The question of history has turned out to be much more delicate. While this is obviously a golden opportunity to bend glass and iron into highly elegant details, it is much harder to control the overall design of buildings. Generally speaking, there are plenty of possible approaches but they are all rather uncertain; a very careful screening of the initial data, a specific agenda set down with great care and a list of well thought-out ideas are not, and never will be, enough to solve the whole matter. Voysey appears to have been quite right: why are all these steps necessary, if not to find the key and set the rhythm of design? At this point, something else must come into play.

GMW's project for the Old Bailey involves, for example, a very cool way of incorporating a relatively small old building, an Edwardian building, in a brand new building (made of glass and iron), actually turning into its head. This coupling together is both bold and blatant. Was there any alternative? Of course. But this is a fine result, the underlying poetics are certainly consistent; in some sense it also indicates a course of action that is somewhere between the old and new. On the other hand, Minster Court shows a marked propensity for Gothic echoes, helped along by a touch of expressionism, rather reminiscent of Lyonel Feininger and also Fritz Hoeger. This leads to quite a few problems: evidently other approaches might have been tried. Nevertheless, it would be nice to think there was a real reason for it: the influence of Pugin (it makes little difference how far back that takes us), who saw something clean and authentic in the Gothic style that justified the resorting to functional architecture. On the other hand, there is Hector Horeau, an architect of iron and glass, and a real believer in progress, who used to draw on Gothic forms.

This was a long time ago. But it gives us something interesting to think about, against a backdrop of feasible prospects for a form of growth that must be both ethically and practically sustainable if it is to exist at all.

Works

Zurich Insurance Company

The building was designed as the UK headquarters of Zurich Insurance who planned to move from London to Portsmouth in line with the government-backed decentralisation policy of the nineteen-seventies. The brief was to match the quality of their European Headquarters in Zurich and provide new offices that would be attractive to staff relocating from central London.

For GMW, the design marked a departure from the strictly rectangular geometry of the nineteen-sixties and early seventies. Taking its cue from the narrow and curving site sandwiched between a railway line and Stanhope Road, the building has a plan based on concentric arcs. In fully utilising the narrow site, the building oversails the pavement at ground floor level and is supported on pilotis to form an arcaded walkway.

The bulk of the 12,000 square metre development is contained on thirteen identical floors, each of which is approximately 15 metres wide by 50 metres long. The tight tolerances required by the curving form, the floor-to-ceiling glazing and floor-zone perimeter air conditioning grilles all pushed contemporary curtain-wall technology to its limit. The sweeping curves that result give a unique quality to the office space and the full-height glazing reveals impressive views over the adjacent Victoria Park and Portsmouth Harbour beyond. Facilities include staff training, a computer floor, dental/medical suite and a restaurant.

The curves of the long elevations are made up of faceted flat panes of bronze-tinted reflective glass in sealed double-glazed units and bronze anodised framing. These form an unbroken skin over the whole of the building, including cores and roof-level plant rooms. The resulting cohesive modular surface emphasises the simple geometric form and the restrained and precise detail conveys an impression of quiet efficiency.

Client: Zurich Insurance Co (UK) Limited
Location: Stanhope Road, Portsmouth, United Kingdom
Use: Offices, computer suite, staff restaurant, dental/medical suite, staff training, basement parking
Gross floor area: 12,000 sq. m.
Completion: 1977
Photographers: Alusuisse, Richard Einzig/Arcaid

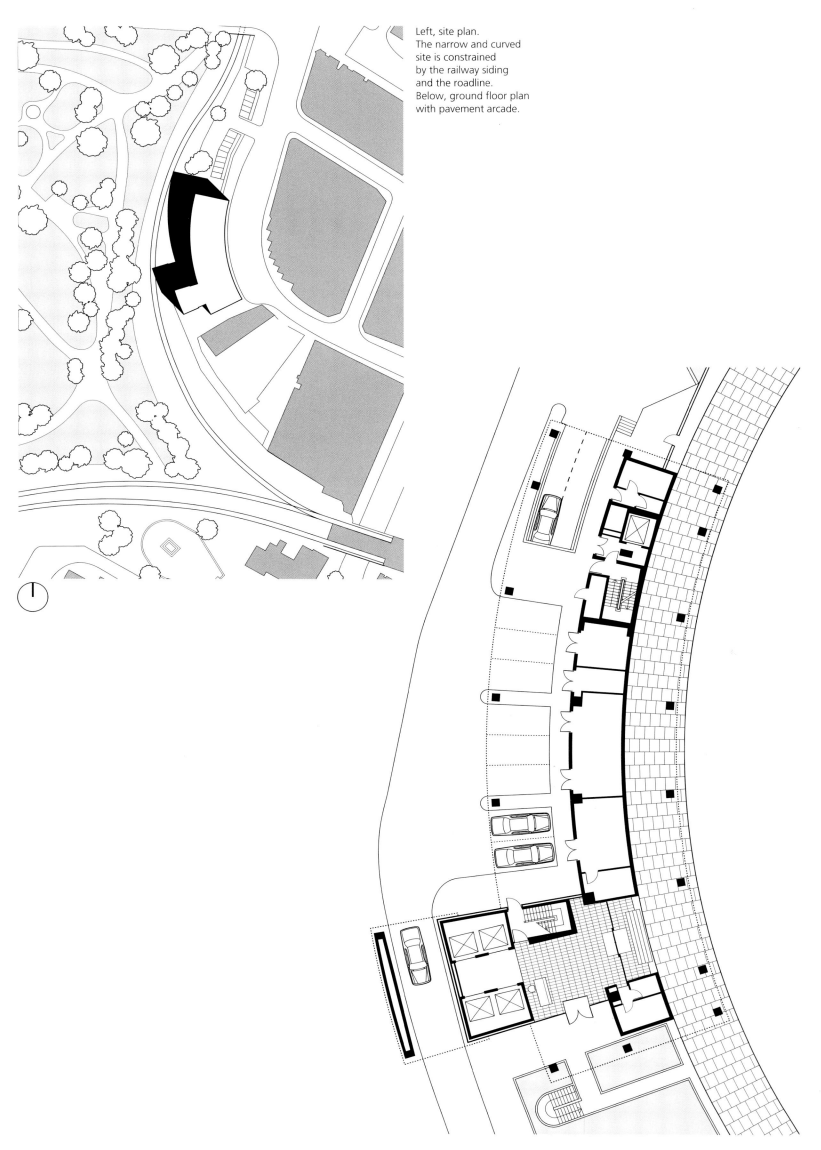

Left, site plan.
The narrow and curved
site is constrained
by the railway siding
and the roadline.
Below, ground floor plan
with pavement arcade.

l'ARCA

11 issues per year
112 pp, colour and
b/w illustrations,
24x34 cm format,
paperback
Languages:
Italian/English
Founded in 1986

l'Arca is an international monthly magazine dealing each month with the most up-to-date realizations, projects, ideas and proposals for contemporary architecture, design and visual communications around the world, presented with the highest full-colour printing and graphic standards. A rich final section is dedicated to News, Information, Events, Exhibitions, Books and Internet Sites Reviews. Subscribers can accede to the magazine in PDF format through the portal www.arcadata.com.

l'ARCAPLUS

4 issues per year
96 pp, colour and
b/w illustrations,
24x34 cm format,
paperback
Languages:
Italian/English
Founded in 1994

l'Arcaplus is a quarterly series of monographs published by l'Arca Edizioni. Each mono-thematic issue collects the best projects and realizations of a special typology or by a protagonist architect on the contemporary architecture scene all over the world.

SUBSCRIBE TO OUR MAGAZINES

HOW TO SUBSCRIBE

SEND A FAX TO NUMBER ++39.02.325481

COMMUNICATE VIA E-MAIL: abbo.arca@tin.it
WITH YOUR OPTIONS, YOUR NAME AND COMPLETE ADDRESS
http://www.arcadata.com

l'ARCAEDIZIONI

Via Valcava 6, 20155 Milano
Tel.++39 02 325246 - Fax ++39 02 325481
E-mail: abbo.arca@tin.it

SUBSCRIPTION FROM ABROAD

Please send me a year's subscription (11 issues) to l'ARCA at the special price of

☐ US$ 130.00 - Euros 134,00 (EEC Countries): Air Mail in Europe and
  Mediterranean Countries
☐ US$ 160.00: Air Mail to USA and Canada
☐ US$ 180.00: Air Mail to Rest of the World
☐ US$ 130.00: Surface Mail

**Please send me a year's subscription (11 issues + 4 issues) to l'ARCA and
l'ARCAPLUS at the special price of**

☐ US$ 170.00 - Euros 175,00 (EEC Countries): Air Mail in Europe and
  Mediterranean Countries
☐ US$ 200.00: Air Mail to USA and Canada
☐ US$ 220.00: Air Mail to Rest of the World
☐ US$ 170.00: Surface Mail
☐ 25% Discount for STUDENTS (Please enclose a copy of your school registration)

☐ First subscription   ☐ Renewal

Name   Surname

Address

Town and Post Code   Country

Profession   Telephone

Fax   e-mail

☐ cheque made out to: l'ARCA EDIZIONI
☐ American Express Card
☐ Diners Club International
☐ Visa   expiry date   ☐☐ ☐☐

n. ☐☐☐☐☐ ☐☐☐☐☐ ☐☐☐☐☐ ☐☐☐☐☐

Signature   Date

Subscriptions will be processed on receipt of payment.
I agree that my personal data are used, as per Law 675/96, for this subscription and relative communications.

Previous page, view south
along the Stanhope Road
frontage.
Below, the office floors
are divided into a mixture
of open-plan and cellular
space.
Right, view from Victoria
Park.

Equitable Life

The form of the Equitable Life building at Aylesbury, completed in 1982, is effectively a cube pushed diagonally from one corner to create inward and outward sloping facades. While this added a formal dynamic to the building it also had an underlying rationale in that south facing facades are shaded and those facing north capture more light.

The deceptively simple shape was realised with no sacrifice of usable space and, in a development of curtain-wall technology, heated mullions counter internal down draughts and obviate the need for perimeter radiators.

Leaning forces are countered by the two vertical cores, which provide circulation between floors, toilets and other services. Externally these cores are clad in warm orange brick, which contrasts with the blue body-tinted glass and blue anodized aluminium of the curtain wall to define a minimalist composition of interpenetrating forms.

The building marks the first inclusion of an atrium in a GMW design. As well as bringing daylight to the centre of the office floors, the atrium is used as a flexible and informal social space at ground level.

Client: The Equitable Life Assurance Society

Location: Walton Street, Aylesbury, United Kingdom

Use: Offices, computer and conference facilities, coffee lounge, restaurant and dining rooms, in-house printworks

Gross floor area: 8,200 sq. m.

Completion: 1982

Photographers: Richard Bryant /Arcaid, Gartner

Left, a suspended
structure has been used
to minimise the visual
presence of the atrium
roof.

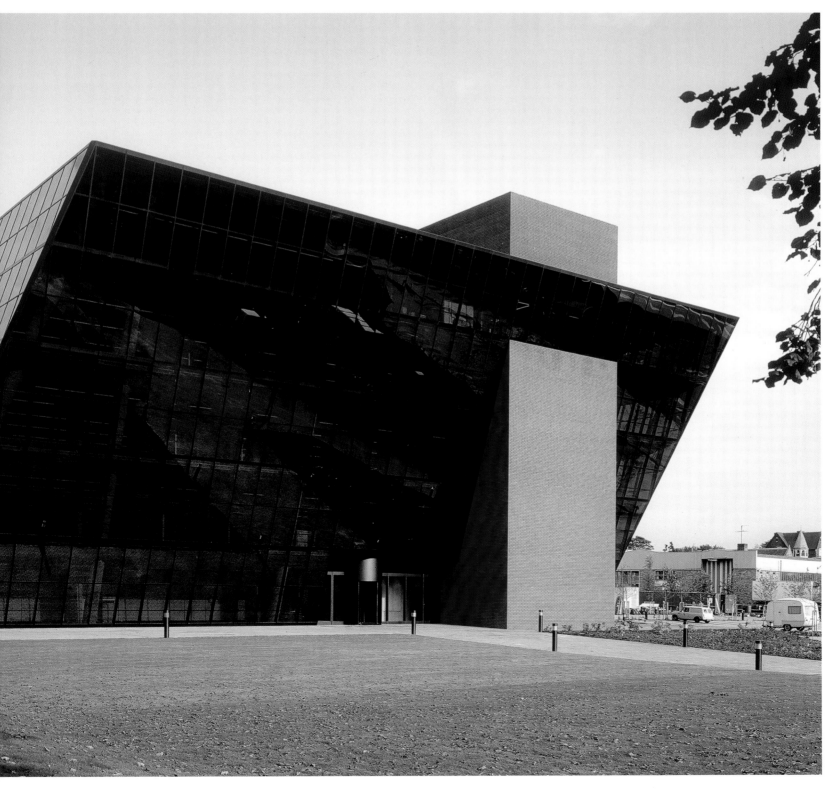

Left and below,
each of the four glazed
elevations slopes at
an angle of 17 degrees
to the vertical.

Left, perimeter columns are parallel to the external walls. Opposite page, the Atrium opens directly onto the reception area and is used for a variety of informal and social events.

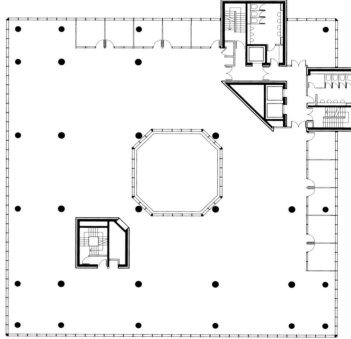

Second floor plan.

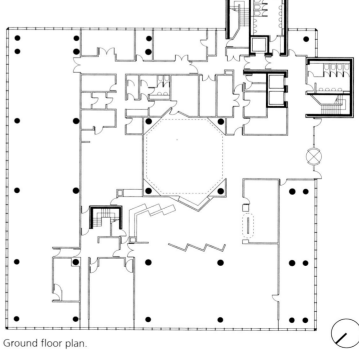

Ground floor plan.

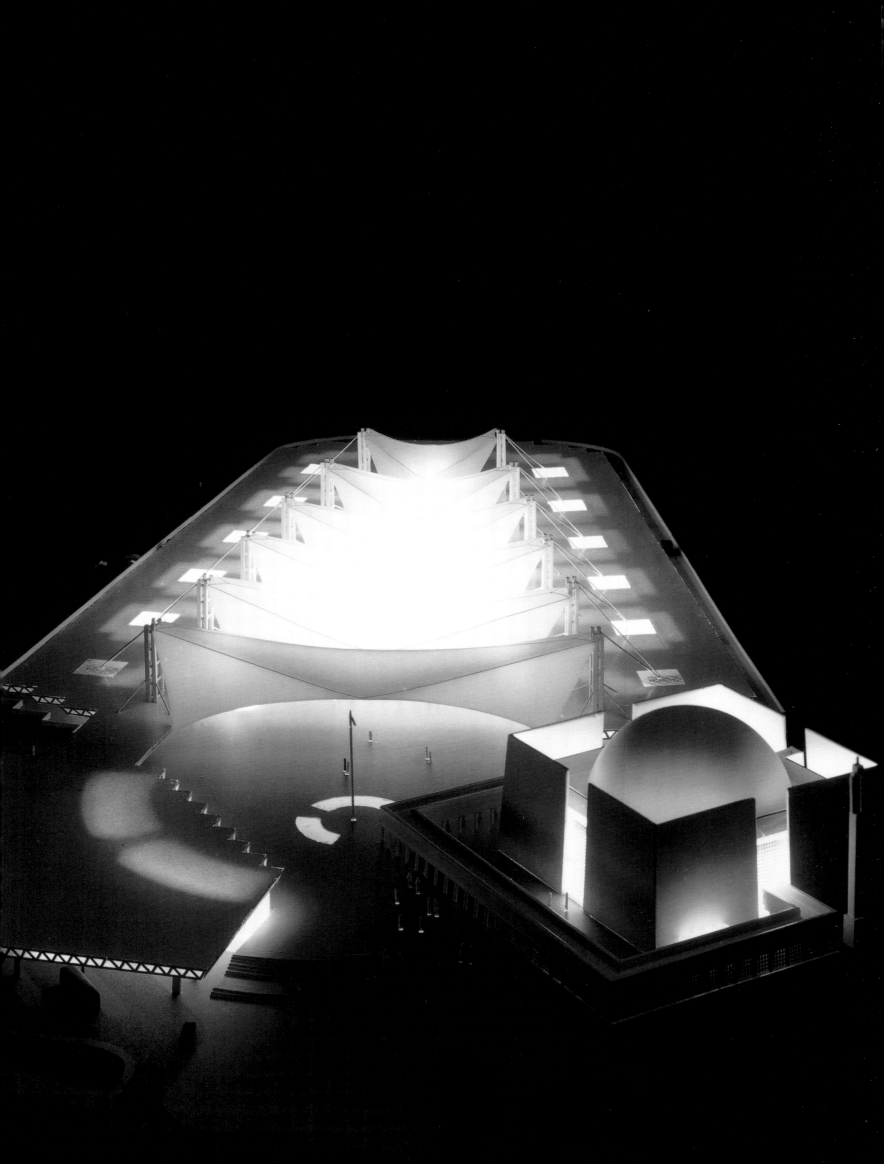

Shandagha Market

The primary urban design objective of this project was to create a new town square surrounded by the three main elements of the complex: the market, the mosque, and the transportation terminal. On the south side of the square, the market units are arranged as a crescent, embracing a large covered public space. The layout of the shop units, serviced entirely from the outer perimeter, generates a series of small-scale and intimate spaces for the buyers.

The lightweight tensile structure over the central public space would greatly reduce solar gain while allowing good natural light. The substantial area of car parking is provided in a controlled environment below the shopping level and within easy reach of various public amenities above. The mosque, which is given a deliberate geometric deflection with its "mihrab" wall facing Mecca, is approached from the town square through a partially covered courtyard.

The project was the winning entry in the international competition invited by Dubai Municipality in 1983.

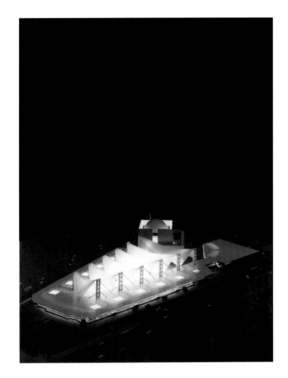

Client: Dubai City Council

Location: Dubai, United Arab Emirates

Use: Retail food market, bus terminal, inter-emirates taxi station, mosque, public car park

Gross floor area: market: 13,500 sq. m., car park: 20,000 sq. m., mosque: 2,500 sq. m., terminal: 4,000 sq. m.

Completion: 1985 (international competition, unbuilt)

Photographer: Ron Margetson

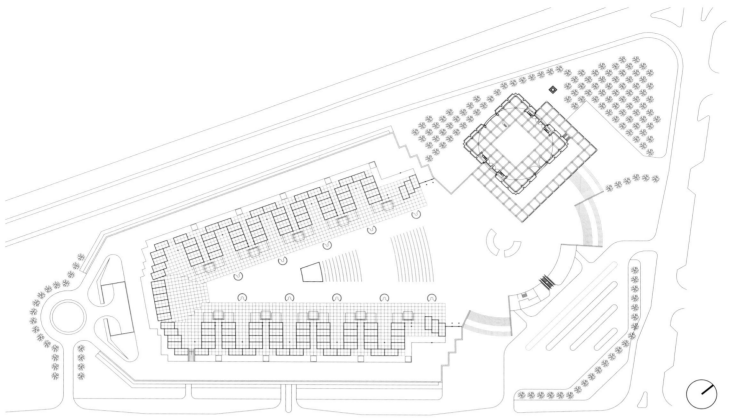

Ground floor plan.

Right, simple geometric forms are used in the mosque.

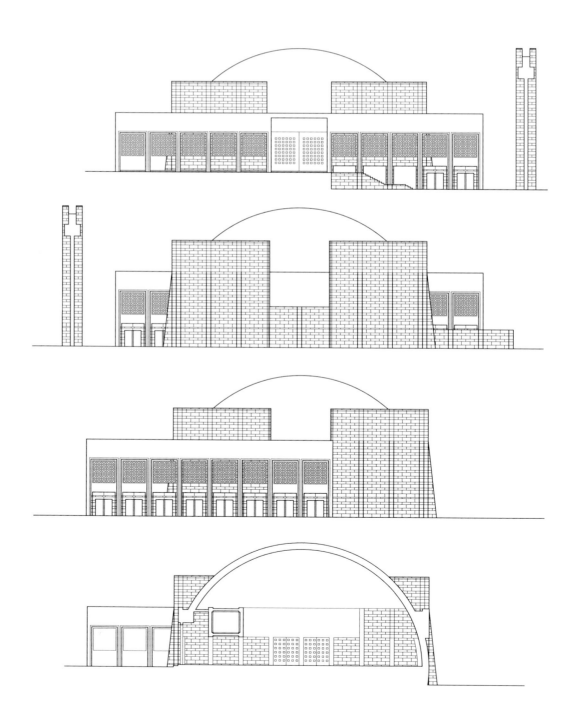

The market units enclose the large public space, which is covered by a lightweight tensile structure.

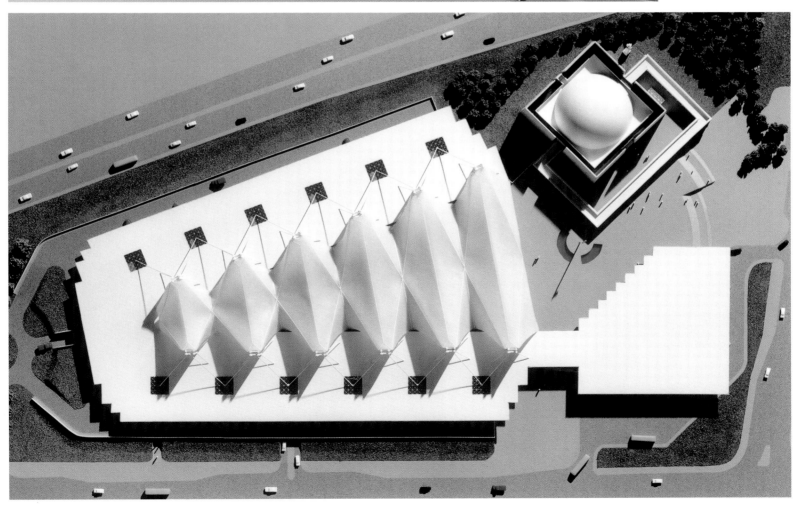

St Enoch Centre

The St Enoch Centre is a unique and heroic response to the complexities of the shopping centre brief. A radical design based on a seven-acre glass envelope resolves a wide range of planning, design and management challenges and gives the Centre a striking visual presence.

The site runs parallel to Argyll Street, one of Glasgow's major shopping venues, and is close to the Clyde waterfront, but was essentially a back-lands area. It had been the site of the St Enoch railway station and the station hotel, which fronted onto St Enoch Square. With station and hotel both demolished, the client sought an urban design and architectural solution that would unlock the potential of the location.

GMW's design met the demand for flexibility in the retail brief and provided vital links to Argyll Street and Lewis's department store. But perhaps the most obvious benefit of the single skin glass canopy is the creation of a naturally lit buffer zone between the Glasgow weather and the fully air-conditioned shop interiors. A combination of passive energy systems keeps temperatures in the mall between a winter minimum of 5º C and a summer maximum of 22º C, providing one of the more enjoyable "public" spaces in Glasgow.

The glass envelope is structurally independent of the buildings within so that radical changes can be made to the layout of the shop units without compromising the exterior of the Centre. In addition to the usual mix of retail units arranged around a three-level mall, the centre opened with a full-size ice rink and a pavement-café style food court.

GMW evolved the design concept and took the lead role in a design team that included Scottish architects Reiach and Hall and retail interiors specialists from HOK of St Louis.

The St Enoch Centre was highly commended in the British Construction Industry Awards of 1990 and was named European Shopping Centre of the Year at MIPIM in 1991.

Client: The Scottish Development Agency for the Church Commissioners & Sears Properties Glasgow Ltd.

Location: St Enoch Square, Glasgow, United Kingdom

Use: Shopping centre with 4 large stores, 70 shops, market area, restaurant, food court, ice rink and public car park

Gross retail area: 27,000 sq. m.

Completion: 1989

Photographer: Alistair Hunter

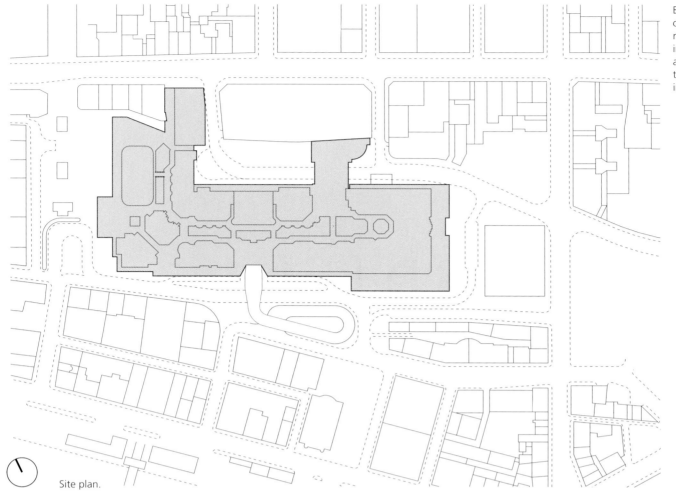

Below, the large expanse of south-facing glazed roof warms the interior in winter and promotes a natural "stack effect" to ventilate the centre in summer.

Site plan.

Vehicle access
to the centre's car park
is via a bridge over
the shopping mall.

Left, tree-head columns
support the longspan
roof structure.
Opposite page, at the top
of the roof structure are
16 pyramids containing
the computer-operated
vents that moderate
the centre's temperature.

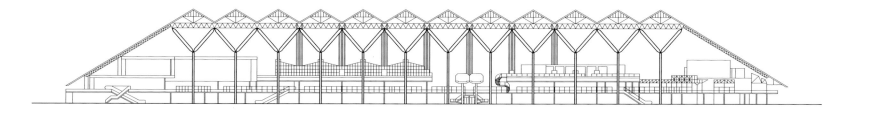

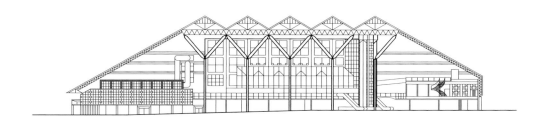

Below, the structure supporting the roof is independent of the retail units and mall beneath. Opposite page, all three levels of the mall are suffused with daylight.

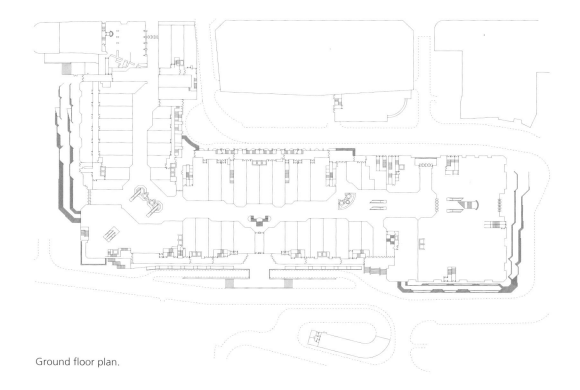

Ground floor plan.

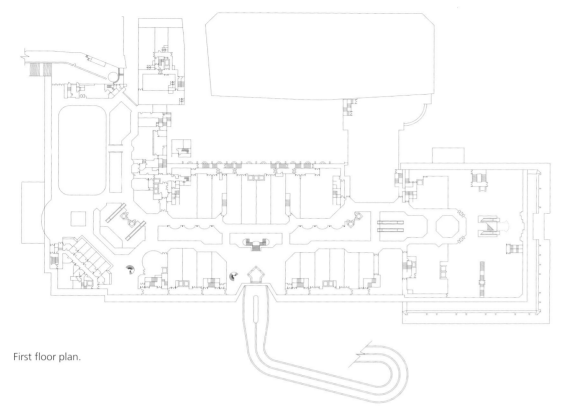

First floor plan.

This page, the design included a food court and a public ice rink, both of which benefited from the centre's moderation of the Scottish climate. Opposite page, the food court has the feel of a pavement café.

Minster Court

At Minster Court, three buildings are grouped around an open glass-roofed court. Elevations are clad in stone, a mixture of polished and flamed granite, and there are references to historical forms. However, the essential expression of the project is of a curtain-wall skin stretched over steel-framed buildings.

Each building is designed to accommodate different tenancy requirements and each has its own formal identity. The exuberant and possibly indulgent details impart unique and particular characteristics to different parts of the buildings. But they also work to unite them within an overall theme intended to combine a new experience with a sense of historical continuity.

The aim was to produce buildings that were in dialogue with their neighbours and which, though large, also related directly to the human scale. The transition from narrow streets to open sky is expressed by window heights that diminish progressively with building height in response to the increased availability of daylight.

The glass-roofed court provides a focus for the three buildings. It is reached via broad steps and gives access to each building a half level above the street. It overlooks Minster Pavement, an intimate space at the heart of the site flanked by cafés, bars and restaurants.

Throughout the project, artwork and sculpture are integrated into the design. The pieces range from the larger-than-life equine statues that signal the formal entrance to the complex, to works that mark individual building entrances and define internal spaces. Together these help subtly blend the public and private spaces into a unified whole.

In this project, GMW explored a contextual and expressionist approach, influenced by the advocates of post-modernism. The articulated forms developed from ideas about how the building forms should address the narrow surrounding streets and the "Gothic" associations that emerged have an underlying humour and rebelliousness that is sometimes misunderstood.

Client: Prudential Portfolio Managers Ltd.
Location: Mincing Lane, City of London, United Kingdom
Use: Offices and restaurants
Gross floor area: 83,610 sq. m.
Completion: 1991
Photographers: Jeremy Cockayne/Arcaid, Chris Gascoigne, Simon Hazelgrove, Richard Leeney, Simon Warren

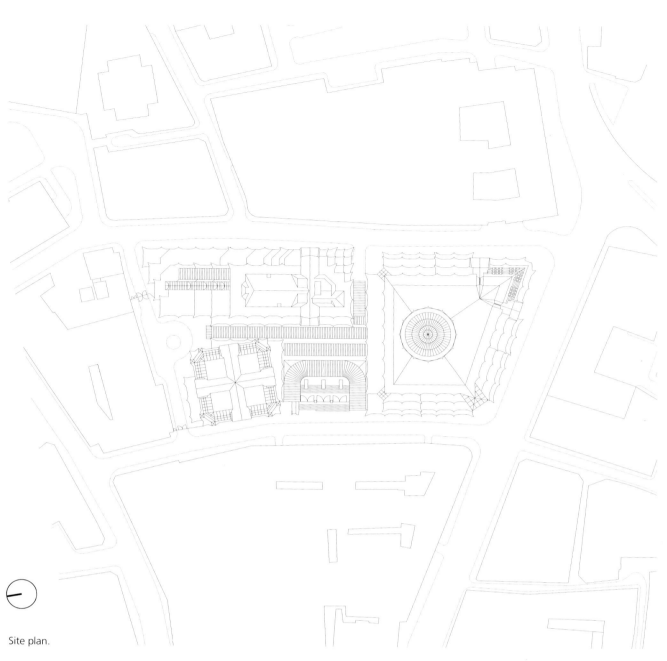

Site plan.

Below, aerial view from
the east.
Opposite page,
Minster Court's distinctive
roofline viewed from
the south bank
of the River Thames.

Left, common spaces throughout the three buildings share a palette of design elements and materials, but are distinguished by individual artworks.

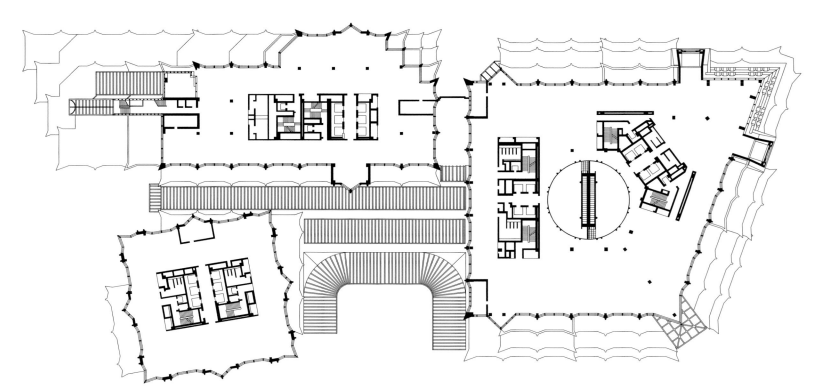

Typical floor plan.

Left, main reception area
in No. 1 Minster Court.
Below, lift lobby in No. 1
Minster Court.

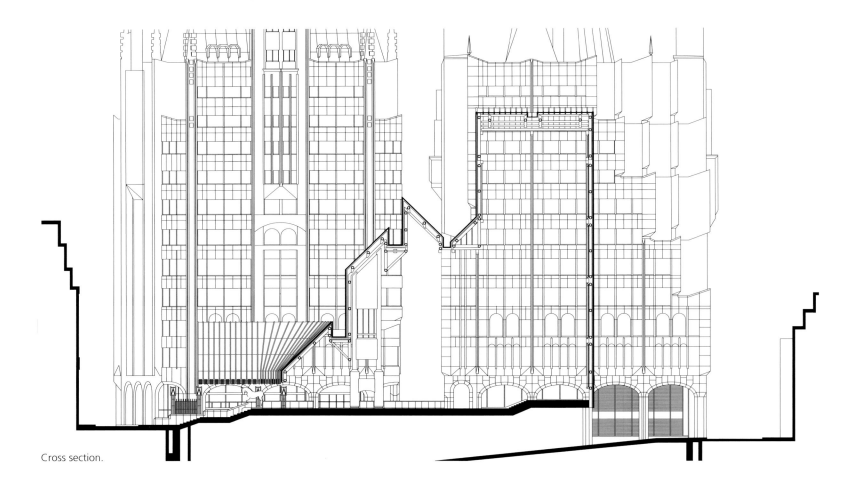

Cross section.

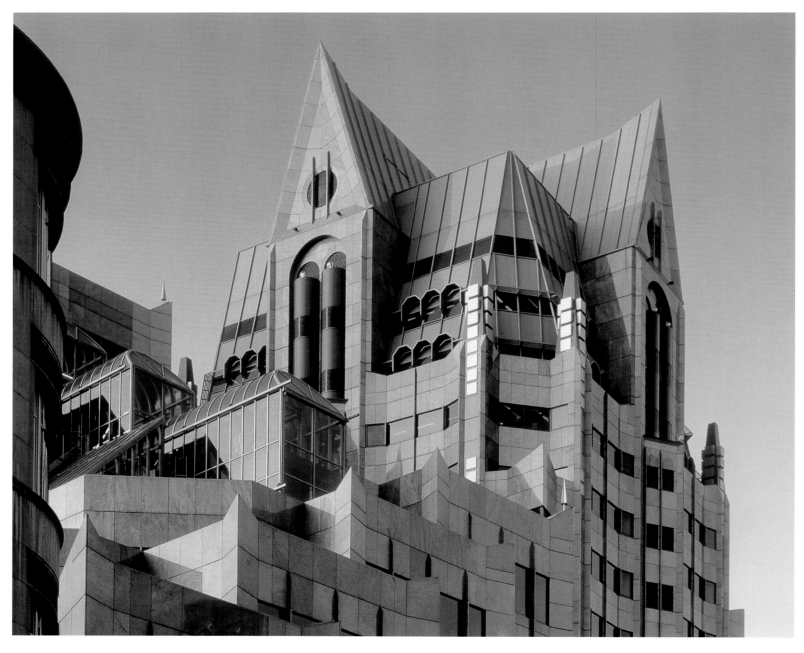

Three, one-and-half times-life size, bronze horses by Althea Wynne mark the entrance to the open court.

54 Lombard Street

54 Lombard Street, built as the headquarters of Barclays, a major UK bank, was a redevelopment of the historical site of the bank. Responding to its location at the heart of London's City financial district, the building volume is divided and articulated with the aim of integrating it into the urban texture of the surrounding area.

The greatest mass of the building is placed on the busiest, broadest street and the form of the building is sculpted to step down towards the network of small-scale medieval alleys and courts that is typical of the interior of many City blocks.

This building marked a departure from the simple geometric forms and minimalist curtain-wall detailing that characterised GMW's previous work.

The design for 54 Lombard Street consciously makes reference to the details of the Edwardian and Victorian buildings nearby in a composition of granite, metal panels and glass. It aspires to a complexity of form and expression based on a belief that a building can have a rich and varied geography of its own, as well as forming an expressive fragment of the city as a whole.

There is a four-storey implied podium at the base of the building. This is clad in light grey granite-faced precast-concrete panels and detailed to reflect the classical elements of the adjoining buildings.

At upper levels the rich modelling of the podium gives way to the smoother more restrained appearance of metal faced curtain walling, a theme of the design being the transition from weight and robustness at street level to lightness at the highest levels. This contrast is emphasised by the division of the tower into three distinct vertical elements rising to different heights.

Each element culminates in a curved profile roof, modulating the skyline of this eighteen-storey building.

Client: Fleetway House Construction Management Ltd.
Location: Gracechurch Street, City of London, United Kingdom
Use: Offices
Gross floor area: 41,300 sq. m.
Completion: 1993
Photographers: Jeremy Cockayne/Arcaid, Peter Cook/View, Richard Turpin, Simon Warren

Above, views of the
entrance area and
ground floor lift lobbies.
Opposite page,
view of the east elevation
to Gracechurch Street.

Fourth floor plan.

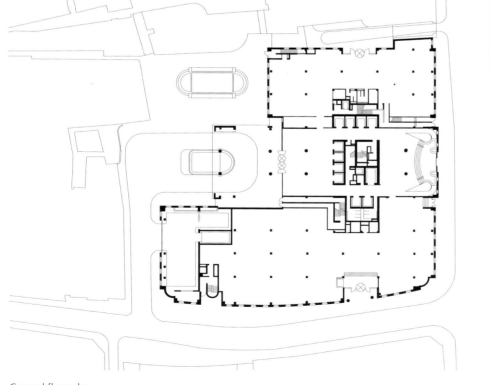

Ground floor plan.

Tower 42

External influences often affect the output of an architectural practice, as does the way one commission leads to another. In April 1992 a terrorist bomb exploded in the City of London and devastated many buildings. GMW had been involved with the National Westminster Bank for some years and had designed out-of-town computer data centres for them. The practice responded swiftly to the Bank's requirement to return the NatWest Tower to operational use as soon as possible. The building, though only completed in the mid nineteen-seventies had become a well-known landmark and in the conservationist mood of the eighties there were those who believed that few, if any more tower buildings would be built in the City. Thus the NatWest Tower might be considered as unique and certainly the Corporation of London Planning Department wished to see it reinstated as originally designed by Richard Seifert.

This wish was acknowledged and although the Tower was stripped back to its concrete structure, it was re-clad to retain the original design. The refurbishment enabled major enhancements to be made to the quality of the office space and added an additional 2,000 square metres of usable area within the original building profile.

While the Tower itself was reinstated, the original small and cramped entrance hall was demolished and replaced with the pavilion illustrated here. It extends from the base of the Tower to the back edge of the footpath, giving the building a strong presence on the street. Its three-storey height is in scale with the adjoining buildings, but is also appropriate to the scale of the tower.

The structure is mainly stainless steel with clear glazing. The external walls are suspended from the roof, which acts as a lattice plate and is supported on only four columns to minimise disruption of three levels of existing basements below.

While providing a dramatic space, the transparent building affords spectacular views of the refurbished tower above, with the cantilevered office floors beginning just a few meters above the pavilion roof and receding into the distance. The tower now has a physical and visual link with the street and an entrance that befits a City landmark.

Client: NatWest Group Property Ltd.
Location: Old Broad Street, City of London, United Kingdom
Use: Offices, restaurants, café
Gross floor area: 61,580 sq. m.
Completion: 1998
Photographers: Peter Cook/View, Anthony Weller/Archimage

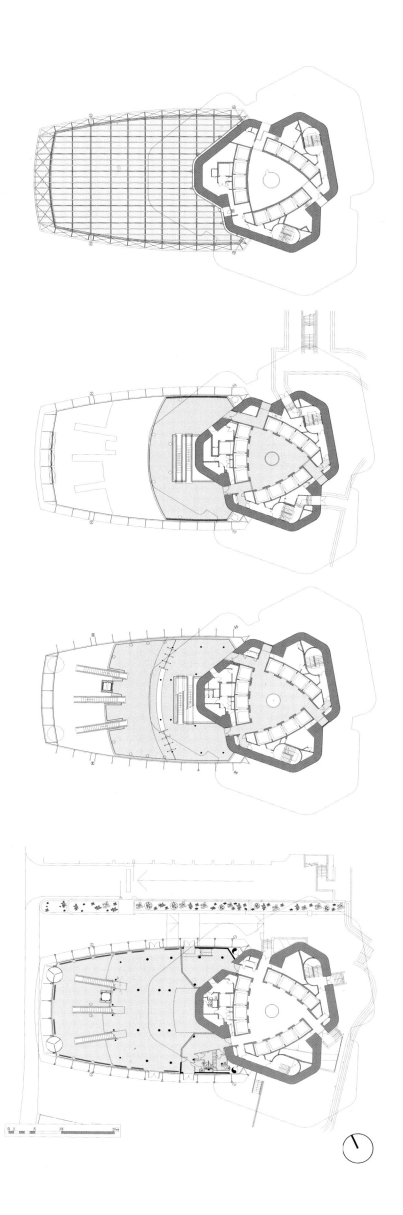

Left, tiered decks
in the entrance pavilion
step back to define
the change from a public
ground level, to the two
secure levels above.
Escalators link all three
levels.

At first level, the custom-designed reception desk incorporates etched-glass panels by Graham Jones.

Right, detail of the suspended structure that braces the single-skin glass façade.
Below, details of the stainless steel structure. Opposite page, four circular columns support the pavilion roof from which the glazed walls are suspended.

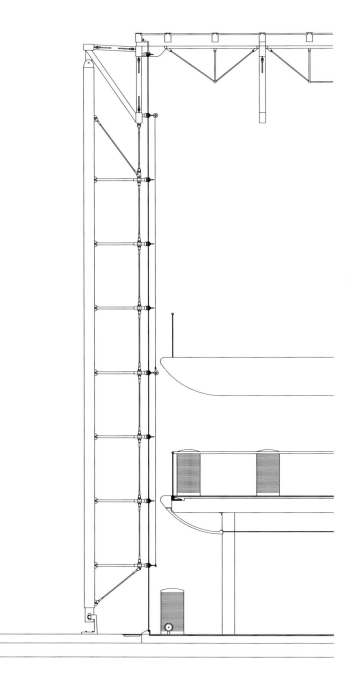

Below, viewed obliquely
from the street, the front
elevation of the pavilion
echoes the scale of the
adjacent buildings.

Opposite page, from
close to, the form and
structure of the pavilion
relates directly to that
of the tower above.

Below, the up-tilted roof
expresses an invitation
to enter.
Right, the transparency
of the structure allows
the form and function
of the entrance pavilion
to be clearly understood.

16 Old Bailey

The redevelopment of 16 Old Bailey combines the historic opulence of a retained Edwardian building with the freshness and precision of a modern office. The design exploits the dynamic interplay between these two elements to create a unique building that is both stylish and efficient.

Located opposite the Central Criminal Court in the City of London, the development site extends from the historically sensitive Old Bailey to a refreshingly contemporary environment in Fleet Place. 16 Old Bailey echoes this transition, with the formal presence of the retained building on Old Bailey, giving way to a sleek modern design along Bishops Court and into Fleet Place. Here a planar-glazed atrium extends the full height of the building and opens up the floors to allow natural light to penetrate deep into the interior. The existing Listed building, formerly called Britannia House, was built between 1912-20. However, with the exception of the retained part, it was of an extremely utilitarian nature and was demolished to make way for the new development.

Extensive new stonework and copper details have been put in place to complete the retained building's composition at the side and rear, where these were incomplete. The distinctive spaces within have been carefully refurbished to enhance their individual character. In particular, the interior of the mansard roof has been opened up to create an impressive double-height space, while the previously solid and inhospitable ground-floor has been opened up with stone piers and glass infill simulating a traditional colonnade. Within this light and open space, a contemporary entrance hall hints at the modern offices beyond.

The main core is situated just behind the reception area and marks the transition between the enclosed spaces of the pavilion and the open office areas facing Fleet Place. Externally the core is clad in opaque black glass using the same frameless curtain-wall system as the office floors. The new elevations have a strong horizontal emphasis that wraps around the Y-shaped floor plan. As the curtain wall passes into the atrium, the horizontal theme of the exterior gives way to larger panels of glass that give a visual openness to the interior space and reflect daylight down into the lower levels.

Client: Hammerson UK Properties Plc.
Location: 16 Old Bailey, City of London, United Kingdom
Use: Offices
Gross floor area: 12,250 sq. m.
Completion: 2000
Photographer: Peter Cook/View

Left, the stonework and copper details of the retained pavilion have been completely refurbished and new hand-carved details added to complete the symmetry of the design. Below, the new implied colonnade at ground level introduces the modern offices behind.

Opposite page, the office floors are arranged around three sides of the atrium. Daylight filters down into the office space despite the proximity of the surrounding buildings.

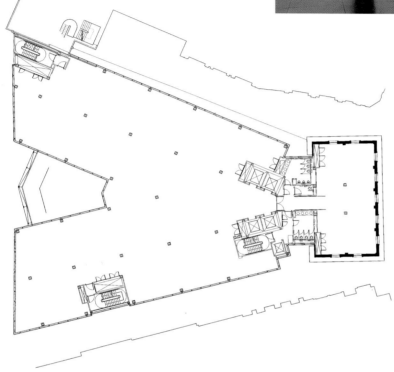

Typical upper floor plan.

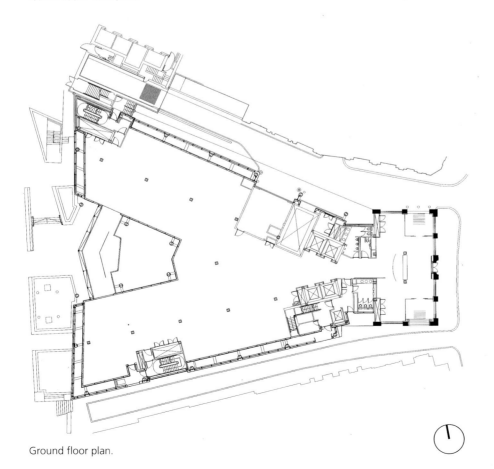

Ground floor plan.

Details of the atrium. Opposite page, the Fleet Place elevation showing the office floors on either side of the planar glazed atrium.

Marathon House

This site was occupied by a tower and podium building designed by GMW for the developer Hammerson in the early 1960s. Some thirty years later, Hammerson wished to replace the functionally outdated building with new offices designed to meet current market demands.

GMW proposed a low rise street-wall building to replace the existing 15 storey tower in a design intended to mediate between two quite different environments; the small scale residential ambience of the Georgian conservation area to the north and the aggressive commercial environment of the heavily trafficked Marylebone Road to the south.

Initially the project was threatened by the potential listing of the earlier GMW building. However, support was gained from the planning officers and this gave us the opportunity to develop the design illustrated here. Eschewing historical reference and earlier minimalism, the design explores a dialogue between organic expression and pure technology. Its metal and glass details are deliberately modulated to suit two very different contextual situations.

The design included a predominantly enclosed northern elevation, sculpted and articulated with textured metal panels and "punched out" windows. This contrasted with a highly glazed southern elevation with outrigged solar-control louvres. The building was designed to act as a foil to the listed library building and registry office on the opposite side of the road while retaining its own identity and presence. A warm, light-coloured finish was proposed for the metal components, with grey tinted glass.

As the design developed, it became clear that the client's ambitions were incompatible with those of the planning committee. The project eventually fell foul of the local authority's mixed-use policy and planning permission was not obtained.

Client: Hammerson UK Properties Plc.
Location: Marylebone Road, London, United Kingdom
Use: Offices
Gross floor area: 18,580 sq. m.
Completion: 1996 (unbuilt)
Photographer: Chris Edgcombe

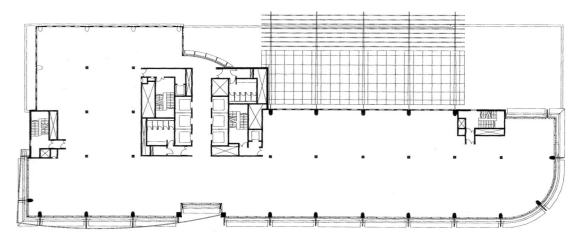

Typical upper floor plan.

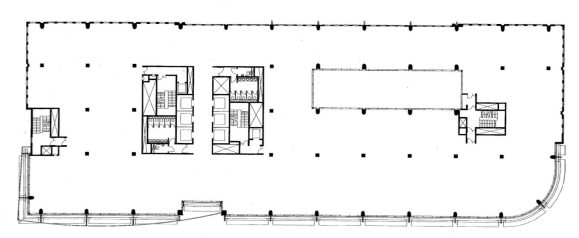

Typical lower floor plan.

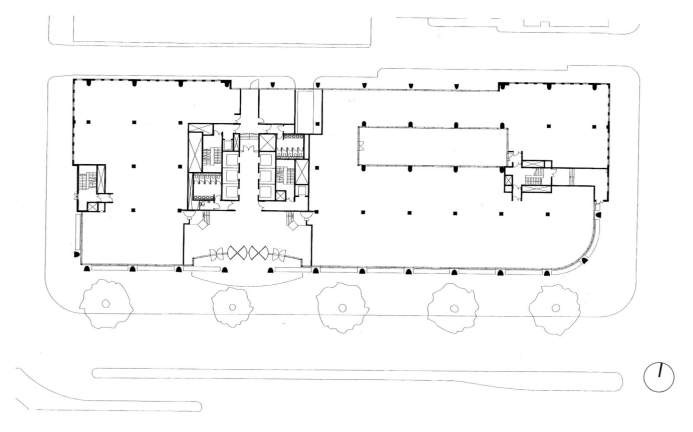

Ground floor plan.

Model of part
of the elevation showing
the solar shading
and the curved
supporting outriggers.

Istanbul, Turkey

Atatürk International Airport

GMW's award winning design for the new international terminal follows the concept of a "box" terminal, with adjacent linear piers. It was inspired by the belief that the form of the building should clearly express its diverse functions, both internally and externally, and within a simple and efficient layout, provide passengers with convenient and instinctively clear routes from the land-side roads to the aircraft and vice versa. This objective is further reinforced by the vertical separation of departing and arriving passengers onto different levels and by the transparency of external facades. The complex includes a 7000-space multi-storey car park linked to the terminal and an underground rapid-transit station to handle the increased passenger traffic. Both the terminal and its pier structures are arranged on three levels, with a spine of service and circulation cores marking the landside-airside boundary. On the airside, a series of distinctive departure lounges, with fully glazed sloping elevations, allow the passengers to enjoy daylight and panoramic views of the aprons. External elevations are clad in silver anodized aluminium and blue tinted double-glazing, and all glazed surfaces are protected against solar gain and glare by deep roof projections and external solar shading structures. The departures area is the defining space of the project. Its 240 metre by 168 metre roof structure, the 'fifth elevation' of the terminal, is easily identifiable from the air and clearly expressed in the interior. The roof structure is a grid of steel and glass pyramids supported on reinforced concrete columns at 24-metre centres. The space beneath floods with diffused daylight through the north-facing triangular skylights and perimeter glazing. This emphasis on natural light has been carried down to the arrivals level with fully glazed corridors along the piers and landscaped courtyards overlooked by the baggage-claim hall. An innovative and award winning design feature of the terminal is the use of seismic isolators placed between the column heads and the large roof structure to protect the building in the event of an earthquake. At the outset, the modular and linear form of the terminal was chosen with expansion in mind. This has proved to be the right strategy, allowing the second phase of construction to proceed with minimum disruption of operations. The design capacity of the terminal is now 20 million passengers per year.

Client: TAV, build-operate-transfer joint venture between TEPE Construction, AKFEN Group and Vienna International Airport.

Location: Istanbul Atatürk Airport

Use: International passenger terminal, multi-storey car park and underground rapid-transit station.

Gross floor area: Terminal: 190,000 sq. m., car park 180,000 sq. m.

Completion: 2000

Photographer: Peter Cook/View

Left, the international terminal with the multi-storey car park to the left and the piers in the foreground, The north-south pier links to the domestic terminal, at the far left in this view. Opposite page, bridge links span the access road and link departures level directly to the multi-storey car park.

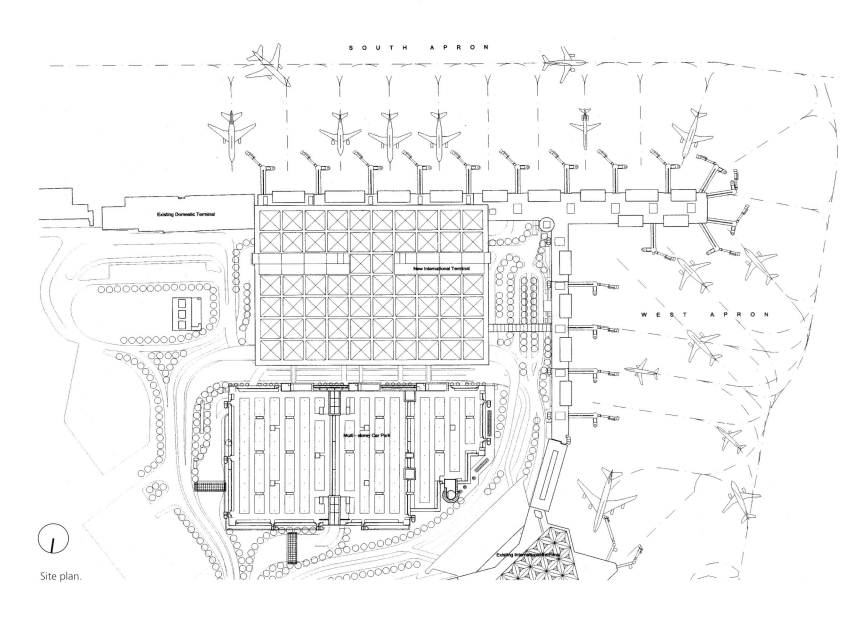

SOUTH APRON

WEST APRON

Existing Domestic Terminal

New International Terminal

Multi-storey Car Park

Existing International Terminal

Site plan.

Left, at either end of the terminal, lifts and escalators connect departures level with arrivals level and the rapid transit station. Below, over the departures level is a grid of steel and glass pyramids supported on columns at 24-metre centres. The generous interior space is flooded with diffused daylight through the north-facing skylights and perimeter glazing.

Opposite page, the eight-metre-wide piers provide access to a series of open departures lounges.

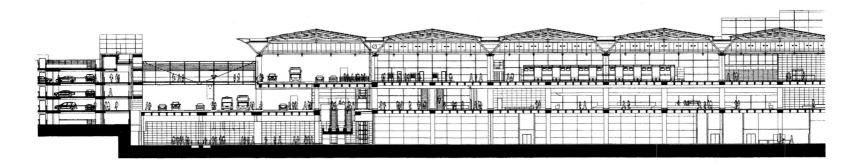

Above, partial
cross-section showing
the horizontal and vertical
links between the
terminal, car park, roads
and rapid transit station
platforms at service level.
Right and opposite page,
Views of the piers from
the apron showing the
departures lounges with
fully-glazed elevations
and solar-shading fins.

Left, landside elevation of the terminal with the apron control tower in the background. Opposite page, airside elevation of north-south pier shows boarding bridge connections to departures lounges at the upper level and the arrivals corridor at intermediate level.

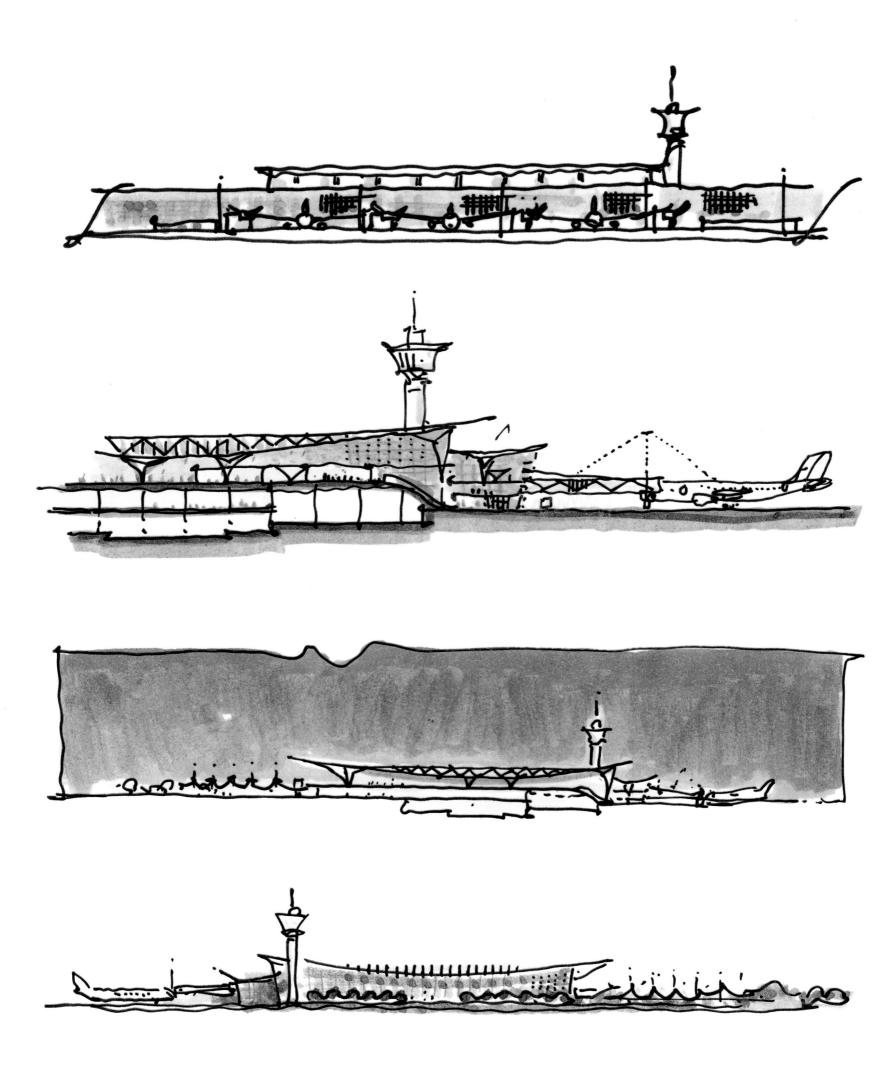

Airport International Terminal

Dalaman Airport serves as the main port of entry to the busiest tourism region in the Turkish Mediterranean and 80% of the 5 million yearly passengers go through the airport in 5 months. Therefore the new international terminal had to have a notional design capacity of 10 million pax.

GMW's prize winning competition entry was based on a composition similar to that of Istanbul Atatürk Airport, also designed by GMW. The terminal is designed as a rectangular building on 3 levels and an adjoining linear pier structure provides 7 contact gates.

A simple and transparent building form was proposed to achieve a light and airy interior, and clear orientation of passengers. Entered from an elevated road, the departures level is roofed over with a large flat deck, strengthened by a series of "folds" at the centre and rising gently towards its two cantilevering edges. Formed by tapering triangular trusses at 16m centres, the "folds" are glazed externally to provide the spacious interior with diffused rays of daylight.

On the land side, a large area is designated to separate zones for cars, taxis and coach parking.

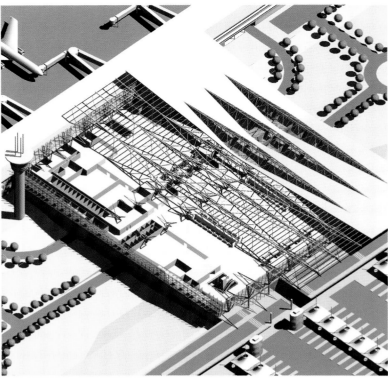

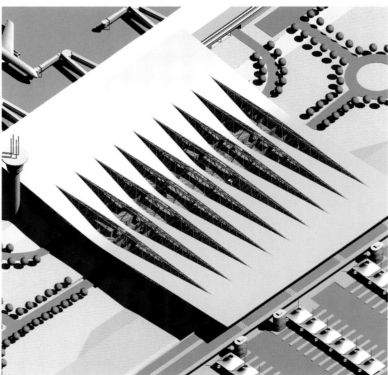

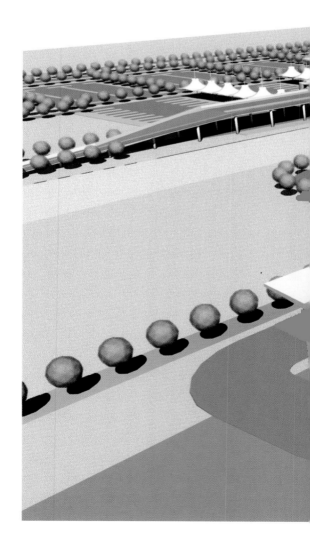

Left, design model of the proposed roof structure over departures level. Opposite page, landside and airside views of the design model showing the proposed massing of the terminal and the adjacent pier.

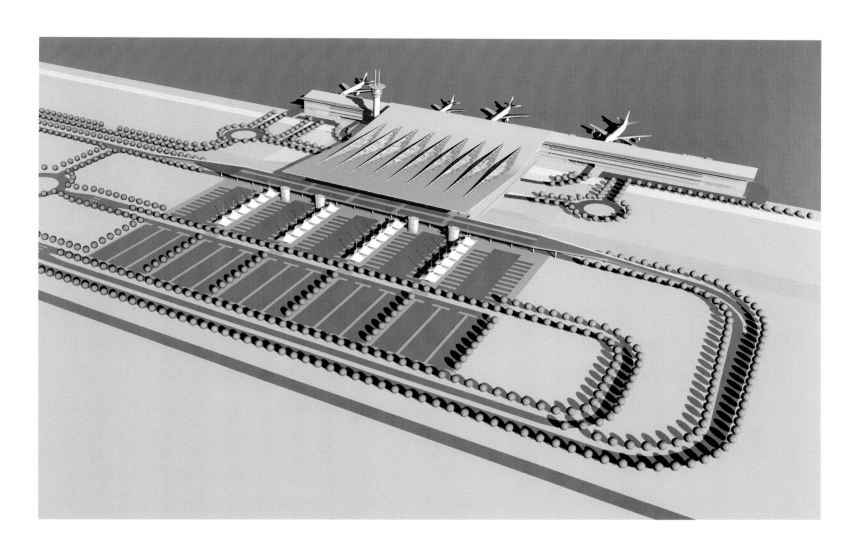

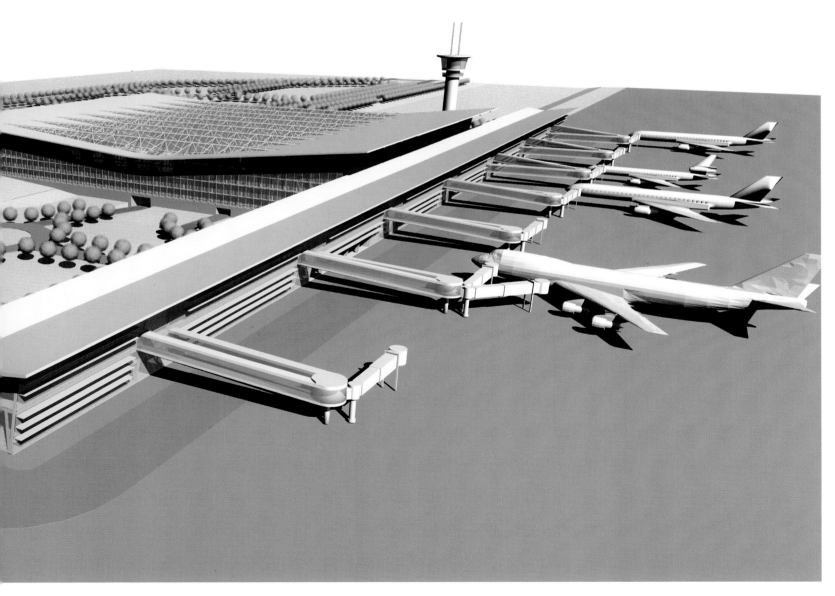

Midsummer Place

Midsummer Place is a major new shopping centre won in developer competition on behalf of London and Amsterdam Properties. The building forms an extension to Milton Keynes' existing shopping centre, which was designed as the core to this well-known British New Town. The new extension is intended to complement the heroic forms of the original with an equally modern, though perhaps freer and more varied series of spaces. The strong expression of the link between Midsummer Place and the existing retail malls gives the project a civic dimension with the intention of encouraging its successful integration into the town.

The construction of the link between the new and existing retail involved the closure of one of the town's main boulevards and the resulting new urban space, called the Boulevard, is covered by an eighteen-metre-high wave form roof.

This is penetrated by four roof-lights and is clear-glazed on both ends. It covers a space the size of a football pitch and is carried by eight columns beneath which are independent pavilions containing shops, restaurants and cafes.

The centre's layout is based on a series of distinctive spaces linked by a circuit of eight-metre-wide malls and walks. These spaces include Oak Court, a large open-air circular courtyard containing the last preserved oak tree in the town centre, South Concourse, which is illuminated by a large south-facing window and links by escalator to the roof-level car parking, and of course the Boulevard itself. The rationale here was to design spaces that had a clear and individual identity and would instil an intuitive sense of place and orientation.

Externally, the building is clad in Spanish limestone above a granite podium, while internally the top-lit malls are finished in white with a muted-grey limestone floor to act as a foil to the colourful new shop fronts.

Part of the fun of the centre comes from the introduction of specially commissioned artwork such as the feature clock by the artist Kit Williams and other sculptural work by local artists. In the large window of South Concourse, a fine stained glass window by Anne Smythe depicts the history of Milton Keynes.

Client: London and Amsterdam Properties
Location: Midsummer Boulevard, Milton Keynes, United Kingdom
Use: Department store, 50 shops, cafés, car park
Gross floor area: 40,000 sq. m.
Completion: 2000
Photographers: Peter Cook/View, Anthony Weller/Archimage

Left, one of the island units in the Boulevard. Opposite page clockwise, the planar glazing to the west elevation of the Boulevard; the Boulevard looking east; view south across the Boulevard towards West Walk with Oak Court in the background.

The Boulevard is a roofed
space that links
Midsummer Place
to the original retail
centre in Milton Keynes.
It has given the shopping
centre a new urban
quality and sense
of arrival.

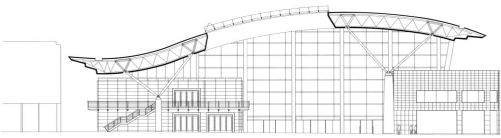

North-south section through the Boulevard.

Opposite page, Oak
Court with its mature oak
tree and the Boulevard
beyond.
Below, the east elevation
of the Boulevard.

List of Works

1949
Bonham Road Residential Development, London

1950
Little Furze County Primary School, Oxhey

1952
St Julians Secondary School, St Albans

1953
Sheffield University Competition

1954
Sheffield College of Technology & Commerce

1955
93-97 New Cavendish Street

1957
118-126 New Cavendish Street

1959
University of Sheffield, Master Plan
St Mary's Hospital, Paddington
Sheffield University Library

1960
Castrol House, London
Radley College - Berkshire
18 Manchester Square, London

1961
Oxford University Pharmacology

1962
Sheffield University Students' Union
Sheffield University - Physics & Maths building

1964
Kettering General Hospital

1965
Sheffield University - Arts Building
Loughborough College

1966
Hillingdon Hospital, London
Equitable Life Offices, London

1967
BOAC Boadicea House, London Heathrow Airport

1968
P&O Building, London
Sheffield University - Chemistry Department
Royal Military College of Science, Shrivenham
South Wales Electricity Board, St Mellons

1969
Commercial Union Tower, London

1970
BA Terminal, J. F. Kennedy Airport, New York
Royal Military Academy, Sandhurst
HMS Caledonia- Rosyth
Post Office Savings Department - Durham
RAF WestDrayton
Desford Upper School, Leicestershire

1971
University of Cambridge Library
Wreake Valley Upper School, Leicestershire

1972
Harold Wood Hospital

1973
Manulife House, Stevenage
Swimming Pool, Woking

1974
Chipperfield School - Hertfordshire

1975
British Steel Computer Centre
Offices and computer facilities at the steel plant in Rotherham

New Covent Garden Market
Relocation of London's main fruit, vegetable and flower markets to Vauxhall, London

1977
Banque Belge
Offices in the City of London

American Express
UK headquarters for Amex in Brighton, clad with innovative GRP system

Zurich Insurance
Offices in Portsmouth

Equitable Life House
Assurance Society offices in Aylesbury

1978
Crown Life House
Assurance Society offices in Woking

Wharncliffe Gardens
Residential development in Central London

1979
Pontings Development, Phases I&II
Refurbishment and extension of retail arcade and offices at Kensington High Street Underground Station

Moi International Airport
New main terminal building at Mombasa's Airport

1980
St Christophers Place & Barrett Street
Master plan and implementation of a regeneration project in London's West End

Harold Wood Hospital
Master plan and individual buildings for a District General Hospital in Essex

1981
Baring Brothers & Co
22 storey office tower in the City of London

Vauxhall Cross Development
Mixed office and industrial development in London

1982
Equitable House, Aylesbury
New office building in Aylesbury for the Equitable Life Assurance Society

Royal Opera House extension
Rehearsal, dressing and administrative facilities at Covent Garden

1983
Octagon Centre
Student Union building at Sheffield University with flexible meeting/performance area, bars and associated facilities

Townsend Car Ferries
Offices in Dover for Channel ferry operator

Sandakan International Airport
Design consultancy for regional Airport in Malaysia

Shell Centre Restaurants
Complete refurbishment of catering and entertainment suites at Shell's UK Headquarters

Phoenix House
Office development in the City of London

Mobil Court
Extension to Mobil Oil's UK Headquarters in the historic Clements Inn, London

Replacement Airport, Hong Kong
Master plan and development studies for the new Hong Kong Airport at Chep Lap Kok. (unbuilt)

King William Street House
Office development in the City of London

Postal Sorting Office
Mechanised sorting office with associated staff facilities and vehicle maintenance workshops for Royal Mail at Nine Elms in London

Dubai Wholesale Food Market
Competition winning scheme for a major new market (unbuilt)

1984
King Saud University
New campus university for 25,000 students in Riyadh, Saudi Arabia

1985
STC factory & offices
Microchip manufacturing plant laboratories and offices in Kent including state-of-the-art clean-rooms and associated plant

Shandagha Market
Competition winning scheme for a major new market, transport interchange and mosque (unbuilt)

City Tower
Complete refurbishment of 1960s office tower in the City of London

1986
Viking House
Offices for Thoresen Ferries in Portsmouth

BOC Group headquarters
Parkland office development at Windlesham

1987
Ergon House
Office refurbishment in London

1988
Nobel House
Office refurbishment in London

IC House
Refurbishment of a 1930s office building in Westminster for ICI

33 Great Portland Street
Mixed use retail, office and residential development in London

1989 & 1990
Axis House & Mondial House
Master plan and first two buildings on an office park at Heathrow, London

1989
Holborn Circus development
Redevelopment proposals for Daily Mirror site in London, taken to planning permission (unbuilt)

Citygate
Office development in Southwark

191 Old Marylebone Road
Office development in Westminster

Sheridan House
Offices in Harrow

St Enoch Centre
Shopping centre in Glasgow

Shell Mex House
Complete refurbishment of 1930s London Headquarters undertaken with the client in occupation

77 Shaftesbury Avenue
Office and retail development in London's West End

1990

Aeropole Charleroi
Master plan for Airport development and office campus at Brussels South Airport

Marlborough Court
Business park office development, Milton Keynes

NatWest Third Data Centre
Computer centre of NatWest Bank in Staffordshire

BT Network Management Centre
Telecommunications control centre in Shropshire

1991

Crossways Business Park
Business park office development, Dartford

Abbey Life headquarters
Insurance company Headquarters in Bournemouth

1 Giltspur Street/18/20 Cock Lane
Offices in the City of London

Eagle House
Offices in the City of London

4-7 Chiswell Street
Offices in London

Minster Court
Three office buildings in the City of London

12-15 Finsbury Circus
Offices in the City of London

Leith House
Offices in the City of London

The Institute of Ophthalmology Stage 4
Teaching and research facilities at Moorfields Eye Hospital in London

1992

Daventry Town Centre Study
Urban regeneration study (unbuilt)

Hill Samuel Bank
Prototype fit out for bank offices, Birmingham

120 New Cavendish Street
Offices in the West End of London

34-35 Leadenhall Street
Offices in the City of London

1993

Copenhagen Concert Hall
Entry to international competition (unbuilt)

20 North Audley Street
Office fit out in London for UK leisure company Bass plc

54 Lombard Street
City of London headquarters for Barclays Bank

1994

First Choice Holidays
Offices at London Gatwick for holiday company

Thames House
Major office refurbishment in Westminster for a government department

1995

Paunsdorf/Hermelinstrasse
Residential development in Germany

99 Bishopsgate
Refurbishment and extension of a 1960s City of London office building damaged by a bomb attack

Citibank, La Plaine
Office fit out for Citibank in Brussels

St Michael's House
Office development in the City of London

1996

Caxton House
Office fit out in London for a government department

University of Greenwich Student Housing
Student housing in South London

Marathon House
Proposed office development in Westminster Scheme taken to planning permission. (unbuilt)

Faraday Complex
Proposed office development in the City of London Scheme taken to planning permission (unbuilt)

Broadway/Carteret Street
Proposed office development in Westminster Scheme taken to planning permission (unbuilt)

1997

Reuters, Gemini Court
Fit out for Reuters in London

Duty and Tax Free Shop
Retail fit out for Alpha Retail at Heathrow Airport

93-97 New Cavendish Street
Office refurbishment in London

Aquis House
Office development in Reading

1 King William Street
Offices in the City of London combing new and retained elements

Regis House
Offices in the City of London overlooking London Bridge

1998

Watchmoor Point, Camberley
Master plan and industrial units in Surrey

NatWest Bank Account Management Centre
Offices and staff facilities in Kent

Citibank, Warsaw
Office fit out for Citibank in Poland

Globe House
Office development in London for Hammerson plc and subsequent fit out for British American Tobacco. Winner of BCO Award in 1999

Tower 42
Refurbishment and extension of the iconic NatWest Tower in the City of London

1999

83 Pall Mall
Office fit out in London

Crest Co
Office fit out for the Bank of England in the City of London

2000

BAT e-Commerce
Innovative office fit out in London, winner of BCO Award in 2001

Millbank Tower
Refurbishment of landmark Grade II listed office tower on the River Thames in Westminster

16 Old Bailey
Office development in the City of London

Gatwick North Terminal APV Facility
New gates and lounges for aircraft on remote stands at London Gatwick Airport

Black Friars Court and Evangelist House
Office and residential developments in the City of London

Istanbul Atatürk Airport
New international terminal for Istanbul's main airport

Midsummer Place Shopping Centre
Shopping centre in Milton Keynes

2001

Gatwick North Terminal IDL extension
Extension to the international departures lounge at London Gatwick Airport

Vodafone
Office fit out in Theale for telecoms company

College of Law, Birmingham
Teaching facilities, library and offices in a converted building

College of Law, London
Refurbishment of teaching and common areas

15-20 Manchester Square
New offices in London

Broadway Square Shopping Centre
Shopping centre in Bexleyheath

Altius House
Award winning fit out for accountants KPMG in Milton Keynes

2002

Public Guardianship Office
Office fit out in London for a government department

The Beacon School
Master plan and extensions to a boys' school in Buckinghamshire

Commission for Health Improvement
Office fit out in London for a government department

Victoria Station Master Plan Study
Study of the commercial and environmental potential of London's Victoria Station and the surrounding area (unbuilt)

5 Billiter Street
Offices in the City of London

Park Lane Hotel
Hotel development at Marble Arch in London

2003

Tropicana Hotel and Villas
Resort hotel and individual villas at Antalya, Turkey

Current

CIPD Headquarters
Offices for the Chartered Institute of Personnel and Development in Wimbledon

41 Lothbury
Refurbishment and extension of offices facing the Bank of England in the City of London

Profile of Firm

The ethos of GMW has always been based on a true collaboration in which individual partners fulfil complementary roles. This approach was established soon after the formation of the partnership in 1947 and from the beginning worked very successfully for founding partners Frank Gollins, James Melvin and Edmund Ward. It has remained a guiding principle through subsequent generations of senior partners and today Terry Brown, Lyn Edwards and Ali Özveren fulfil complementary roles in a similar way and each bring their own perspective to the direction of practice.

The early work of Gollins Melvin and Ward set the practice on a path from which it has not strayed far over the years. Buildings worked on in the early days such as those at Sheffield University and Castrol House are viewed with some nostalgia and a great deal of respect, especially in the light of today's renewed confidence in the forms (if not the principles) of modern architecture. It is good for today's partners to recall working directly with those responsible for the pioneering projects.

Including the founding three, there have in all been some nineteen partners, of whom the current senior partners represent a fourth generation. Roughly half were charged with design responsibilities and they in turn, have been supported by many other designers within the practice. While the partners have changed, the practice has retained its identity, though the name was modified following the originator's retirement from Gollins, Melvin and Ward to the GMW Partnership and more recently to GMW Architects.

Gollins Melvin and Ward were a hard act to follow and the current partners of GMW admit that such a successful and well-known heritage can be something of a mixed blessing. Notwithstanding, they have been determined to sustain and build on design excellence through a process of constant renewal from project to project. In recent years, the partners and staff of GMW see themselves as a community of designers, visualisers, technicians and project co-ordinators who strive for excellence in the built product, but who are committed to the idea of teamwork.

While specialising according to their natural inclination, today's senior partners also share management responsibility, which is worked through with other partners and senior staff in regular face-to-face meetings. Lyn Edwards explains:

"For some years now my role has been orientated towards the more commercial aspects of winning and setting up projects, client liaison and strategic business development. This usually requires contact with projects from inception to completion, which can be demanding on time and memory. Whilst there are good days and bad, overall I still have the energy and a strong desire help lead the practice through to continuing success.

My greatest satisfaction is derived from the creation of good buildings. That some are landmark buildings significantly contributing to the urban environment, often heralded as icons, is particularly gratifying."

The current senior partners are intent on looking into all aspects of the way the practice works. They see a need to keep abreast of changes in client organisations and in the building industry. While they can draw on a wealth of experience, they have to ensure that this can be used effectively when tackling new projects. This they see as part of the attention to continuity and succession that has long been a mark of the practice. Master and apprentice work together, combining new with tested ideas, in the light of a mature but challenging critique.

GMW adopts a systematic approach to design, which pays off handsomely when large or complex projects are tackled. Believing strongly in design management, they aim to treat a project in depth, think laterally, test mercilessly, but avoid mind numbing box ticking. The design process, they believe, demands a fine balance between visionary excitement and dogged rigour. Ali Ozveren puts it this way:

"I like to define design, in its broadest sense, as an intellectual and artistic activity that aspires to create objects with desired properties.

I think that the design process should aim to arrive at the optimum solution through a balanced combination of systematic thinking and inspired intuition. Systematic thought begins with the formulation of the design brief, which should encapsulate the client's objectives, the relevant design criteria and the specific functional environmental and economic constraints.

One of the most crucial pursuits in architecture is 'design integrity'. By this I mean continuity, consistency and harmony. Particularly in large and complex buildings, overall design success can only be achieved through a fully integrated approach and continuity in the design process. Design activity starts with a blank sheet of paper and does not come to an end until the last construction detail is resolved and the fittings and fixtures are selected."

GMW's approach to architecture focuses on people's aspirations and needs. The point is made that, because buildings are an integral part of everyday life, it is important that they be comfortable, convenient and inspiring. Buildings are potentially a source of personal delight, a stimulus to more effective working and a strong expression of community or corporate culture. This conviction, that architecture can be instrumental in establishing quality of life for everyman, is a legacy of Modernism that is a real inspiration to GMW's designers. Terry Brown explains:

"Architecture is a social art that focuses on the creation of sheltered, facilitated and serviced places to serve human activity. It is also a 'fine' art in that buildings are symbols and especially for the urban dweller, the very stuff of our physical and sensory experience. It is these environments: buildings, spaces, gardens, streets, cities, that are important, both as the topography of our lives and as the expression of identity and ideas.

Design is no more than the process of visualizing futures, postulating possible new environments and drawing up the necessary plans. But the plans have to be feasible, affordable and ethically acceptable and the futures attractive and sustainable."

The act of drawing is central to the culture of architecture, but the T-square and set square have mostly given way to the computer. An early start with computers means that for GMW, drawing and visualising using the computer is second nature. The use of CAD modelling and, increasingly, animations is now a normal part of design technique. There will always be a place for hand drawing though. In fact the excitement and directness of freehand drawing has been combined with computer use in both two-dimensional and three-dimensional work using a host of hybrid techniques.

There have never been rigid divisions within the practice. The partners, between them, run all projects and tend to concentrate on either design or management, though this time honoured distinction is becoming increasingly blurred. Interior design has always been a strong aspect of the service and the interiors group has a definite identity within the practice. It currently accounts for roughly a fifth of workload.

GMW now sees its service as comprising four interrelated and mutually supportive elements: urban design, architecture, interior design and project services. This, the partners maintain, offers the rounded service that clients now seek. In a world of proliferating specialists, the architect must be an expert generalist with a confident designer's overview. As it develops and more sophisticated design tools become available, the designer has to be ever more alert to the possibility of inept, or worse, incompetent work.

Though it has often been involved with international projects, GMW has generally worked out of a single office in the United Kingdom. For the last fifteen years or so, the base office has been in Kensington High Street, London. Following the success of the competition winning International Terminal at Atatürk Airport, GMW has opened an office in Istanbul. GMW Architects is also the founding practice of the European Architects Alliance, an association of architects across Europe that shares specialised project expertise and offers a wealth of international experience to clients who wish to cross national boundaries.

Considering their reputation, Terry Brown says, "It is true that GMW Architects is regarded as a commercial practice. But this essentially means three things to us. Firstly that we work mostly in the commercial sphere, producing buildings that either support business or are designed to accommodate business activity. Secondly, that we are team workers who acknowledge the importance of time schedules and budgets. But thirdly, that we operate to the high standards of design and professional service that commercial sector clients demand."

At the time of writing GMW comprises about one hundred personnel. In the United Kingdom they are regarded as a large practice. While numbers have inevitably fluctuated over the years, project teams have been carefully structured so that partners remain closely involved in both the design and management of all jobs.

It will be clear from the dates given above that the period covered by this book saw three generations of senior partners. Brian Mayes, Bob Headley and Robert Smith retired in 1989 and were succeeded by Julian Ryder Richardson and Neil Southam. The current senior partners took over in 1997. There have been many and varied working relationships between the personnel of GMW on the projects included here. In the years following the departure of the founding partners, a culture of anonymity grew up and authorship of the various projects was rarely individually credited. GMW now acknowledges the importance of individuals and the human mark that makes each project unique. They have also become more relaxed about the dynamics of belief, opinion and approach out of which their projects are born.

GMW knows only too well that, within the multi-disciplinary design teams of modern commercial projects, the architect has to work hard to sustain the integrity of his design concepts. There is sometimes not much room for subtlety in design ideas that have to be swiftly communicated and easily assimilated. In a world where buildings are seen increasingly as a short life commodity, the partners believe that clients should be persuaded to take the long-term view. The careful, problem-solving approach to design that is a keynote of GMW's service will ensure that issues such as this and, no less, the choice between different futures that each design project raises, will always be thoroughly aired.